CHRISTMAS

Joanna Ponto and Arlene Erlbach

Enslow Publishing
101 W. 23rd Street
Suite 240
New York, NY 10011
USA

enslow.com

Published in 2017 by Enslow Publishing, LLC.
101 W. 23rd Street, Suite 240, New York, NY 10011

Library of Congress Cataloging-in-Publication Data

Names: Ponto, Joanna, author. | Erlbach, Arlene, author.
Title: Christmas / Joanna Ponto and Arlene Erlbach.
Description: New York, NY : Enslow Publishing, [2017] | Series: The story of our holidays | Includes
  bibliographical references and index. | Audience: Grades 4-6.
Identifiers: LCCN 2016001027| ISBN 9780766076198 (library bound) | ISBN 9780766076174 (pbk.) |
  ISBN 9780766076181 (6-pack)
Subjects: LCSH: Christmas--Juvenile literature. | Christmas--United States--History--Juvenile
literature.
Classification: LCC GT4985 .P58 2016 | DDC 394.2663--dc23
LC record available at http://lccn.loc.gov/2016001027

Printed in the United States of America

To Our Readers: We have done our best to make sure all websites in this book were active and appropriate when we went to press. However, the author and the publisher have no control over and assume no liability for the material available on those websites or on any websites they may link to. Any comments or suggestions can be sent by e-mail to customerservice@enslow.com.

Portions of this book originally appeared in the book *Christmas: Celebrating Life, Giving, and Kindness* by Arlene Erlbach.

Photo Credits: Cover, p. 1 DNY59/E+/Getty Images; p. 4 iStock.com/jabejon; p. 7 Image Source White/Thinkstock; p. 9 ASphotowed/iStock/Thinkstock; p. 13 Christopher Furlong/Getty Images News/Getty Images; p. 16 Suzanne Tucker/Shutterstock.com; p. 17 © AP Images; p. 20 © North Wind Archives; p. 22 CandyBox Images/Shutterstock.com; p. 24 Nagel Photography/Shutterstock.com; p. 26 kanphoto/Shutterstock.com; p. 27 Bennett Raglin/Getty Images Entertainment/Getty Images; p. 29 © Karen Huang.

Craft created by Sophie Hayn and Aniya Strickland.

Contents

A visit to Santa
gives kids a chance
to say what they
want for Christmas
that year.

Chapter 1

Christmas Day Is Coming

For millions of people, December 25 is a day they look forward to all year. That day is Christmas, one of the most celebrated holidays around the world.

Preparing for the Big Day

As Christmas gets closer, many children and their families begin to prepare for the holiday. Some write letters to Santa Claus in hopes that he will bring them gifts. More than four billion Christmas cards are sent to friends and family in the United States each year.

At school during December, children create projects featuring Christmas themes. They may participate in holiday assemblies. Some children collect clothes or food to give to the needy. Many schools close between Christmas and New

Santa Claus, Indiana

There is a town in Indiana called Santa Claus. At the town's entrance there is a giant statue of Santa Claus. It is 25 feet (7.6 meters) tall and weighs about 40 tons (36 metric tonnes). Each year the post office in Santa Claus, Indiana, gets about five million pieces of holiday mail.

Year. Children often attend class parties, which may include gifts or a visit from Santa Claus.

Celebrating Christ's Birth

Christmas customs differ from place to place and family to family. Some people put up a Christmas tree right after Thanksgiving. Others wait until Christmas Eve, the day before Christmas. Many exchange gifts and attend church services on Christmas Eve, too.

During the weeks before Christmas, many homes are decorated. They might display nativity scenes that depict the birth of Jesus, who was born more than two thousand years ago.

No matter how people celebrate, they share a tradition with many people all over the world. They are honoring the birth of Jesus Christ, the founder of the Christian religion. The word *Christmas* means "Mass of Christ."

Families prepare for Christmas by decorating their Christmas tree with lights and ornaments.

Chapter 2

The Meaning of Christmas

Even though Christmas is celebrated in December, nobody knows for sure the date of Christ's birth. His birth date was based on a different calendar than the one we use today. He may have been born during another month of the year.

Christ Is Born

What we do know about Christ's birth comes from a part of the Bible called the New Testament. According to the story, a couple named Mary and Joseph lived in the village of Nazareth. The town is now part of Israel. At that time, Nazareth was part of an area known as Judea, which was ruled by Romans.

An angel told Mary she would have a baby. The baby would be named Jesus, and he would be God's son. Mary and

Joseph needed to travel to Bethlehem, a town about 100 miles (161 kilometers) from their home. Mary and Joseph planned to sleep at an inn when they reached Bethlehem. But the inn had no room for them. Instead, the innkeeper allowed them to stay in the stable.

Mary gave birth to her baby in the stable. She used a manger, a feed box for animals, as his bed. A star appeared in the sky. Three magi, or wise men, followed the star to Bethlehem and brought gifts for the baby. Angels told shepherds about the birth of Jesus. The

To celebrate the story of Jesus's birth, nativity scenes are displayed throughout the season.

shepherds came to the stable to see him. Then they spread the news about the birth of God's son.

The Beginning of Christianity

When Jesus grew up, he became a preacher. He told people to love one another and that they should be kind. He healed the blind and the sick. People who believed that Jesus was the son of God became his followers. His twelve closest followers were called apostles. They taught his lessons to many people.

Not everyone believed that he was God's son. Pontius Pilate, the Roman governor of Judea, feared that Jesus might lead a revolt against the Romans. Jesus was arrested for his teachings and then crucified. He was nailed to two wooden poles that formed a cross, and he remained there until he died. His body was then placed in a tomb. The Bible tells that Jesus came back to life for several weeks. Then he rose to heaven to be with God.

After Jesus's death, many people followed Christianity, the religion that he had founded. But many early Christians followed pagan traditions, too. They believed that more than one god controlled natural events, such as daylight, weather, and the seasons.

These people observed both their old pagan festivals and the newer Christian celebrations.

Pagan Holidays

Christian priests wanted Christians to stop celebrating pagan holidays. They wanted the people to celebrate only Christian holidays. Christmas seems to have replaced pagan festivals that ancient people held in late December. These holidays honored the return of the sun.

For people who live in the Northern Hemisphere, winter begins on December 21 or 22. The first day of winter is the shortest day of the year. This is because Earth is at a point where it is tilted farthest away from the sun, and less sunlight

Measuring Time by Christ's Birth

Many countries count time starting from the birth of Christ. The United States is one of the countries that uses this system. The years after Christ's birth are noted by the letters AD. This stands for Anno Domini. It means "in the year of our Lord." The letters BC after a year stand for "before Christ."

In recent years, an alternative reference has been used more. Many people use CE, which stands for "common era," and BCE for "before common era."

reaches Earth. As winter approaches, the hours of daylight shorten. A few days after winter begins, Earth tilts closer to the sun and begins to receive more sunlight. Then the days become longer.

Some people who lived long ago thought the sun might not return. They held festivals honoring the gods that they believed controlled the sun. People hoped that by doing this, the sun would return.

Romans held a festival called Saturnalia. It honored Saturn, the god of farming. It ended on December 25 with a holiday called the Birthday of the Unconquered Sun. During Saturnalia, people held feasts and gave gifts. Northern European people celebrated a similar holiday called Yule. Persians honored Mithra, the goddess of light, at this time of year.

December 25 Is Chosen

Many early Christians celebrated holidays honoring the return of the sun and the birthday of Christ. They did not always observe Christmas in early winter, though. Some people celebrated Christmas in the spring.

About three hundred years after Christ's birth, Christian leaders in Rome said the date for Christ's birthday should be December 25.

December 25 was already a holiday in the Roman Empire. Church leaders probably hoped that Christians would stop celebrating that holiday and celebrate Christmas instead.

Gradually, people began celebrating Christmas instead of honoring the return of the sun. But they celebrated Christmas differently than we do now. Christian priests wanted it to be a day for prayers, not a day to have fun.

These people dress up as ancient Romans and celebrate Saturnalia to honor the god of farming.

Chapter 3

A Giving Holiday

If Christmas is to celebrate Christ's birth, then why do we give gifts to each other? The idea of giving gifts at Christmas was part of the earlier holidays honoring the return of the sun. Christian priests did not like this idea. Gift giving was a symbol of the holiday they wanted Christians to replace. But people did not stop giving gifts. Eventually, the tradition of gift giving was connected to a man named Saint Nicholas, later known as Santa Claus.

Saint Nicholas

Saint Nicholas was a Christian bishop. He lived around 300 CE. He was known as a friend to sailors, the poor, and children. After his death in 343 CE, he was remembered for his good deeds and was made a saint.

December 6, the date of Saint Nicholas's death, became a holiday in many parts of Europe. Children left their shoes by their fireplaces on the evening of December 5. They believed that Saint Nicholas would ride across the sky on his horse and carry gifts for good children. In the morning many children found candy and toys in their shoes.

Santa Claus

During the mid-1500s, a new kind of Christianity spread throughout Europe. It was called Protestantism. It was led by a man named Martin Luther, who did not like the worship of saints. He disliked Saint Nicholas Day because it was in honor of a saint. He also thought the customs of Saint Nicholas Day were childish. Many of his followers thought that children should still receive gifts, though. But

Early Children's Toys

During the 1700s, most children's toys came from Europe or were homemade. Toy companies in America began to open in the 1800s. Children no longer had to wait for the latest toys to be shipped all the way from Europe. Things like dolls, balls, and tin animals were popular toys.

they thought the gifts should come from a figure more closely related to Christmas.

In some countries, new gift givers took the place of Saint Nicholas. They were more closely related to Christmas. In Germany, the Christ child, known as Christkindl, brought gifts to children. In England, children received gifts from Father Christmas, a large man dressed in a red robe lined with fur. French children called him Pêre Noel, which means "Father Christmas" in French. Saint Nicholas was still the gift giver in the Netherlands. Dutch children called him Sinter Klass. This is where we get the name Santa Claus.

In 1624, Dutch people settled in what is now New York. They brought their Saint Nicholas customs with them. Some forty years later, the British took over the colony. They also brought their Christmas customs, including Father Christmas. Father Christmas brought gifts to British children. Saint Nicholas brought gifts to Dutch children. Eventually, the Dutch and British people began to marry each other, and they shared customs. Gradually, Sinter Klass and Father Christmas were blended together into one gift giver, Santa Claus.

The Christkindl (*center*) is celebrated during the holiday season in festivals and markets.

Chapter 4

The Holiday We Know Today

In the United States, Christmas was not widely celebrated until the late nineteenth century. Before then, it was not a legal holiday. Children attended school that day and their parents went to work. Some people believed that Christmas celebrations were sinful. Not everyone in the United States knew about Santa Claus.

The Night Before Christmas

An author named Clement Clarke Moore and an artist named Thomas Nast helped to shape the idea of Santa Claus and the holiday we know today.

While riding home in a sleigh in December 1822, Clement Moore got the idea for a poem about Christmas. He called his poem "A Visit From Saint Nicholas." You may know this poem as "The Night Before Christmas." One of his friends liked the poem. She sent a copy of it to a newspaper in Troy, New York.

Close to Christmas Eve in 1823, the newspaper published the poem. Over the next few years, the poem was printed in many newspapers. Millions of people were able to read it, which helped the tradition of Santa Claus to spread.

Between 1863 and 1886, Thomas Nast drew pictures of Moore's creation each year for *Harper's Weekly* magazine. This helped to make Santa Claus famous all across the United States.

Christmas Trees

The custom of decorating evergreen trees began in Germany around the 1600s. Soon the custom spread throughout Europe.

In 1850, an American magazine printed a picture of Queen Victoria, the queen of England, at Christmas. Her family stood around a Christmas tree. The tree had been decorated by her husband, Prince Albert, who was born in Germany. During the

Thomas Nast illustrated this depiction of Santa Claus preparing to travel down a chimney on Christmas Eve.

Poinsettia

The plant called poinsettia reminds us of Christmas. It became popular during the 1800s. It is named after Dr. Joel Poinsett. He saw the plants during a visit to Mexico. But many poinsettias are also grown in parts of the United States.

1800s, many German people came to live in the United States and they kept this tradition.

Christmas Cards

The idea of sending Christmas cards began in the early 1800s in England. English schoolboys sent out decorated paper greetings, called Christmas pieces, to their parents. These showed how well the boys could write. The boys hoped their good handwriting would earn them many Christmas gifts.

In the 1840s, the English postal service improved, and it became easier for people to mail cards and letters. One of the officials at the post office had a friend named John Horsely, who published children's books and was also an artist. In 1843, Horsely designed and printed about one thousand cards with Christmas themes. They sold well. Soon many companies began printing Christmas cards.

The first Christmas cards to be sold in the United States came from England. In 1875, a man named Louis Prang began printing Christmas cards in Boston, Massachusetts. Soon he was selling one million cards every year. Other companies copied his cards.

By 1890, the idea of Christmas as a festive holiday was accepted by most people in the United States. It was also a legal holiday in all states and territories by 1890.

Sending out Christmas cards is a way to send well wishes to friends and family.

Chapter 5

Celebrating Christmas

People celebrate Christmas in many different ways. Some like to remember the religious origins of the holiday. Others celebrate the spirit of Christmas.

The Advent Season

Many people go to church services on Christmas Eve, Christmas Day, and throughout the Christmas season. Many Christians mark the season of Advent, the four weeks before Christmas. They create an Advent wreath of evergreens with four candles standing in the greens. They light one candle on each of the four Sundays before Christmas as they wait for the holiday.

The Secular Side of the Holiday

Many people also celebrate the secular, or nonreligious, aspects of Christmas. They enjoy the holiday without going to church. They like the feelings of family, kindness, and caring that Christmas is all about. Many modern songs, stories, and movies about Christmas focus on these things.

Most churches are decorated for Advent, the four weeks before they celebrate the birth of Jesus.

In 1949, the song "Rudolph the Red-Nosed Reindeer" was recorded. The song is about a reindeer who is teased because he has a big red nose. It is a popular Christmas song that helps us think about being kind to all people, including those who are different. "I'll Be Home for Christmas," another song, expresses the idea of wanting to be with one's family during Christmas.

There are many other traditions about Christmas that aren't necessarily religious. Some families have gift-wrapping parties, while others decorate cookies or bake gingerbread. See the recipe on the next page to try making gingerbread yourself! Others enjoy caroling, or singing traditional songs, for their neighbors. Christmas means different things to different people.

Christmas Tree Farms

Most Christmas trees come from tree farms. They take five to fifteen years to grow. More than thirty million trees are sold in the United States each year.

Christmas Gingerbread*

Ingredients:

½ cup (95 g) vegetable shortening
½ cup (100 g) white or raw sugar
1 egg
½ cup (120 mL) dark molasses
1½ cups (180 g) all-purpose flour
¾ teaspoon (3¾ mL) baking soda
½ teaspoon (2½ mL) baking powder
1 teaspoon (5 mL) each: ground
  cinnamon and ground ginger

½ teaspoon (2½ mL) each: ground
  nutmeg and ground allspice
pinch salt
½ cup (120 mL) warm water
whipped cream for topping (optional)

Directions:

1. Preheat oven to 350° F (175° C).
2. Grease a loaf pan by rubbing the inside with a stick of butter or spraying it with oil. Then dust the pan with flour and shake it until flour has covered every surface of the interior.
3. With an electric mixer, beat the shortening and sugar together until it is fluffy and light in color.
4. Add the egg and molasses and mix thoroughly.
5. Sift the flour, spices, salt, baking soda, and baking powder so no lumps form.
6. Gradually add the dry ingredients into the batter. Alternate with the warm water. Mix on medium speed for about one minute once all ingredients have been added.
7. Bake 35-40 minutes or until a toothpick comes out clean from the center.
8. Top with whipped cream and serve warm.

* Adult supervision required.

The Reason for the Season

People often say that too many people think of Christmas as a time to spend money on gifts instead of

Christmas carolers entertain those celebrating the season.

thinking about the reason Christmas was started. It is true that Christmas decorations may appear in stores as early as September, three months before the holiday. And people in the United States do spend a lot of money each year on Christmas gifts.

However, the true spirit of Christmas does still exist. Families get together. People give their time and money to help those in need. Many children and adults sing Christmas carols at hospitals and nursing homes. Sometimes they bring baked goods and gifts.

At Christmas, many people try to be kinder and more giving to one another. They think about what their friends and families have meant to them throughout the year. These acts of kindness and generosity are what Jesus wanted to teach. It is fitting that people do these things at the time that they celebrate his birth.

Christmas Craft*

Reindeer remind us of Christmas. After all, they pull Santa's sleigh! Here is how to make a reindeer ornament to hang on your tree, decorate your home, or give as a gift.

Here are the supplies you will need:

clean sticks from ice-cream bars or
   craft sticks
white glue
plastic wiggle eyes
a small red pom-pom
glitter
a 6-inch (15-cm) piece of string
one brown pipe cleaner, cut in half

Directions:

1. Glue the ice-cream or craft sticks together in the shape of a triangle. This forms the head of the reindeer.

2. With one point of the triangle facing down, glue eyes onto the top two points.

3. Glue the pom-pom onto the bottom point of the triangle to make the nose.

4. Cover sticks with glue. Sprinkle on glitter. Let the glue dry.

5. Wrap the pipe cleaner loosely around your finger, molding it into a spring shape. Glue the pipe cleaners to the back of the top of the ornament.

6. Tie both ends of the string together. Glue it to the top of the ornament.

Reindeer Ornament

*Safety note: Be sure to ask for help from an adult, if needed, to complete this project.

Glossary

bishop—A high-ranking official in the Catholic Church. He is selected by the pope to be the leader of a local church community.

Christianity—The religion that Jesus Christ founded.

Christmas Eve—The night before Christmas.

manger—A feed box for animals.

nativity scene—A Christmas decoration that shows the birth of Christ in the manger.

pagans—People who believe in more than one god.

saint—A holy person or a religious hero who sets an example for others.

shepherd—Someone who takes care of sheep.

Learn More

Books

Archer, Mandy. *Christmas.* Hauppauge, NY: Barrons Juveniles, 2013.

Bruna, Dick. *Christmas.* London, England: Simon & Schuster Children's, 2013.

Pettiford, Rebecca. *Christmas.* Minneapolis, MN: Jump!, 2015.

Trueit, Trudi Strain. *Christmas.* New York, NY: Children's Press, 2013.

Websites

Christmas Crafts at Activity Village
activityvillage.co.uk/christmas-crafts
   Scroll through a huge selection of Christmas crafts for kids of all ages.

Santa Games
santagames.net/santa/intro.htm#content
   Have fun playing games about Santa Claus and Christmas!

Website of the North Pole
northpole.com
   Send a letter to Santa and find Christmas craft ideas, gift ideas, and recipes.

Index